The Arrernte Landscape

A guide to the Dreaming tracks and sites of Alice Springs

By David Brooks for Mparntwe people

Illustrations by Shawn Dobson

IAD Press
Alice Springs

ACKNOWLEDGEMENTS

Most of the information contained in this book was passed on to me by the Aboriginal custodians of Mparntwe (Alice Springs) during the period 1984 to 1987 when I worked for the Aboriginal Sacred Sites Protection Authority. In particular I thank members of the Stevens, Stuart and Rice families, Wenten Rubuntja, Mort Conway and Harold Ross. I also thank the Authority for assisting me and for its work in support of the custodians of Mparntwe and other areas over the years. The idea of this book and the subject matter it covers has been discussed with custodians on several occasions. Details have been checked for accuracy and to ensure that cultural constraints on access are not breached, but it is always possible that someone has a different view or that a story or place name has more than one version. I hope not to cause offence and apologise if I do. The project though modest in scope has been enjoyable.

Thanks go to Shawn Dobson for the illustrations and to Brenda Thornley for the cover design and skyline profiles; also the Promotions and Cultural Development Section of the Aboriginal and Torres Strait Islander Commission for financial assistance with the first edition.

©1991 Institute for Aboriginal Development
First published in 1991 as *The Arrernte Landscape of Alice Springs*
Reprinted 1995, 1996

ISBN 0 949659 62 2

IAD Press
PO Box 2531, Alice Springs, NT 0871
Phone: 08 8951 1311 Fax: 08 8952 2527

Designed by Brenda Thornley
Printed by Gillingham Printers, Adelaide

CONTENTS

Introduction 1

Anzac Hill 4

Annie Meyer Hill 14

References 24

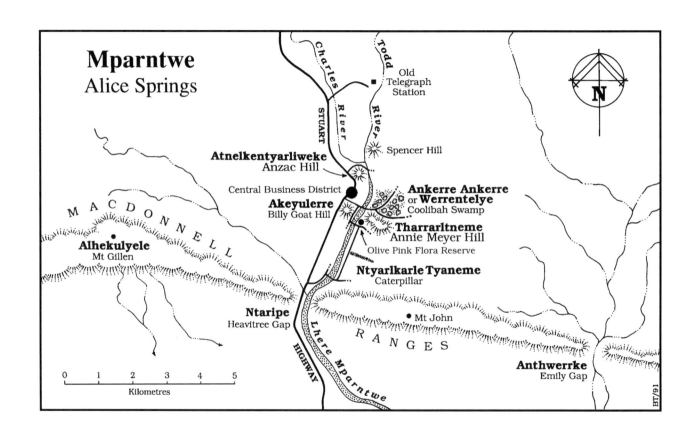

Mparntwe
Alice Springs

Charles River

Todd River

STUART

Old Telegraph Station ■

Spencer Hill ☀

Atnelkentyarliweke
Anzac Hill

Central Business District

Akeyulerre
Billy Goat Hill

Ankerre Ankerre
or **Werrentelye**
Coolibah Swamp

Tharraritneme
Annie Meyer Hill
Olive Pink Flora Reserve

M A C D O N N E L L

● **Alhekulyele**
Mt Gillen

Ntyarlkarle Tyaneme
Caterpillar

Ntaripe
Heavitree Gap

● Mt John

R A N G E S

HIGHWAY

Lhere Mparntwe

Anthwerrke
Emily Gap

| 0 | 1 | 2 | 3 | 4 | 5 |

Kilometres

BT/91

INTRODUCTION

In 1927 Spencer and Gillen, the famous ethnographers of the Arrernte people, published an account of the 'totemic topography' of Alice Springs, pointing out the locations of various sites by means of a series of strip plans. Some of these plans were drawn while the artist was standing on what he called the 'flats at Alice Springs' and for others the vantage point was the top of Anzac Hill. The overall effect was that the viewer took in a 360 degree sweep of the skyline and of all the terrain in between. One of the points made by Spencer and Gillen was that every part of the topography, each creek and hill and peak in the ranges had a name and a 'totemic' association, meaning an association with one or other of the ancestral beings which in Arrernte tradition originally travelled through the area creating the features.

This observation about the density of the Aboriginal significance of the Alice Springs locality well precedes the era of disbelieving developers! Spencer and Gillen displayed a strong sense of admiration for the richness of the culture they were documenting and no doubt expected that future townspeople would be proud to preserve it. This has hardly been the case, as **Mparntwe** (Alice Springs) traditional

1

owner Thomas Stevens has shown in his book *Damaging our Dreaming Land.* Nevertheless, the totemic geography still marks the landscape as strongly as ever. An awareness of even a little of this living topography enhances one's aesthetic appreciation of the beauty of the Mparntwe environment and creates a feeling of empathy with the culture of the Arrernte custodians. In this booklet we introduce the interested observer to a few of the sites which are of significance to contemporary Mparntwe traditional owners. While there are deeper levels of knowledge applying to these sites, it is hoped that the cultural information provided here will give a worthwhile insight into the Arrernte worldview. Some of the sites mentioned are the same ones that Spencer and Gillen wrote about, but others are included as well. Thorough though they were, those researchers certainly did not learn everything there was to know!

We shall be looking here not only at the 'totemic' significance of places but also at the story of their protection or otherwise under the regime of the town. We can only add briefly to the work begun by Thomas Stevens in the book mentioned above. This is an important subject which will no doubt be researched fully in due course, but in the meantime it is important for us to realize that the struggle by Mparntwe people to protect their places is now an integral part of the significance of those places. It is also a critical part of Mparntwe people's history, throughout the twentieth century, for it represents the effort to retain the foundations of spiritual life in the face of almost overwhelming odds.

To follow the text of this booklet it will be necessary to climb Anzac Hill, and then Annie Meyer Hill which provides an excellent view over the eastern side of the town area. It is no good going to look any more from the 'flats at Alice Springs': with the area covered by the buildings of the Central Business District, visibility is rather restricted!

ANZAC HILL

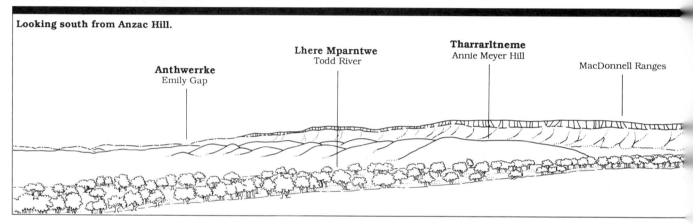

Looking south from Anzac Hill.

Anthwerrke
Emily Gap

Lhere Mparntwe
Todd River

Tharrarltneme
Annie Meyer Hill

MacDonnell Ranges

We begin our overview of Mparntwe from the top of Anzac Hill. Pick out the Todd River passing through the town area to Heavitree Gap which is due south of where you stand. Now look eastwards along the Heavitree range until you see the dip formed by **Anthwerrke**, or Emily Gap. This site, possibly the most important place in the whole region, is where the caterpillar beings of Mparntwe originated.

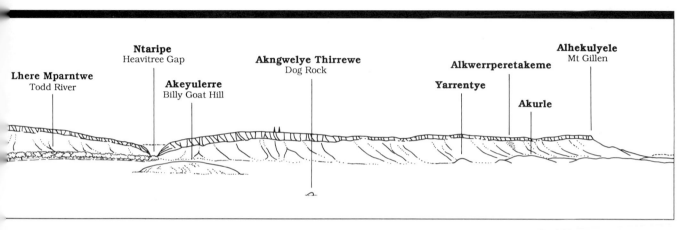

Ntaripe
Heavitree Gap

Akngwelye Thirrewe
Dog Rock

Alhekulyele
Mt Gillen

Lhere Mparntwe
Todd River

Akeyulerre
Billy Goat Hill

Alkwerrperetakeme

Yarrentye

Akurle

The caterpillars are the major creative ancestors of Mparntwe, though as we shall see, many other sorts of beings shaped parts of the landscape, including wild dogs, euros, travelling uninitiated boys, two sisters and kangaroos.

When they had created Anthwerrke, the caterpillars spread out in the general direction of the town area. As they moved they produced the topographical features that we now see, sometimes shaping them by physical means, sometimes calling them into existence by naming them. There were times when they acted more like humans than caterpillars; for instance, we find that certain hillocks and outcrops were formed after the beings (still described as caterpillars) ate the choice parts of members of the species and tossed pieces aside. Then again, on occasion the beings would sit down at a certain spot and paint themselves with red ochre and fat, thus setting the pattern for subsequent ritual performed by people.

There were three species of caterpillar involved, the **Yeperenye, Ntyarlke and Utnerrengatye**. These creatures can be found today, in season, on their respective plant hosts in the region, though Arrernte people say they have declined in numbers since many of the sustaining rituals that used to take place in the town area have had to be abandoned.

The caterpillars (particularly the Yeperenye) are the most important ancestral beings for the Arrernte people of Alice Springs, but the sites associated with them are mainly concentrated on the east side of the town and are best viewed from the top of Annie Meyer Hill. Before we turn to them in the second half of this booklet, we will look over the rest of Alice Springs from our current vantage point.

Ntaripe (Heavitree Gap) is probably second in importance only to Emily Gap, in the context of the Mparntwe area. In 1897 the anthropologist Spencer was shown three storehouses of sacred objects here, but by the time he returned in 1926 they had all been taken by white people. There are several ancestral associations at Ntaripe, including the green beetle Irlperenye, the caterpillars, kangaroo and uninitiated boys. The major one however is the wild dog (Akngwelye).

As well as Ntaripe, most of the features of the Mt Gillen ridge (including the peak **Alhe-kulyele**) were formed by the activities of the wild dog. Indeed, much of the west side of Alice Springs has this association. The story involves an extended battle between a local dog and an interloper from the west, or in some versions from the south-east. They fought over a female, whose cave (and resting place to this day) is up on the main ridge at the green patch called **Alkwerrperetakeme**. During the fighting, a lot of hair (**Akurle**) came

Mt Gillen

off and this now comprises the prominent hill on the flat below the ridge. The local dog also wounded the outsider and some nearby outcrops (**Yarrentye**) were formed from its intestines. From this area the fighting raged to Heavitree Gap, where the intruder was finally beaten and buried.

Partly because of the presence until recently of men's sacred objects, the Gap was traditionally never approached by women, who took a major detour if they were traversing the region. Men also employed great care in using the area, and even now no one ventures up the slopes of the adjacent range. As Alice Springs came to be opened up by the early white people, some of the younger Aboriginal women began to tentatively pass through the Gap – keeping at first to the eastern wall – and now of course they use the route regularly, though a female anthropologist noted recently that when doing so they often lower their voices and eyes, and show apprehension (Rowell, 1981).

Although sites such as those mentioned here undoubtedly represent the valued cultural heritage of Aboriginal people, this may reflect only one side of the picture. Many sites threaten spiritual danger, and custodians feel a heavy responsibility to ensure observance of the rules which keep such forces in check. When people

(Aboriginal or otherwise) ignore or flout these concerns it can cause great alarm and distress.

To return to the wild dog creator being. After defeating his antagonist at Heavitree Gap, he travelled on for only a short distance and then metamorphosed into a boulder embedded in the ground just this side of **Akeyulerre** (Billy Goat Hill), the prominent hill in the middle distance. This boulder (**Akngwelye Thirrewe**) was protected by a chain and marked with a plaque many years ago while it was within the precincts of the railway. Before Europeans arrived, it was the subject of ritual activity involving the application of fat and ochre. Because of the accident of its position, it was one of the first Alice Springs sites to become unusable for ceremony. Several years ago the custodians sought to have the site incorporated within a larger open space area, but instead of this it now sits just outside the front door of a fast

Dog Rock

9

food outlet, the ownership and name of which has been observed to change with bewildering rapidity.

Linked with this site are a number of aggregations of small rocks in the area below Anzac Hill, on the western side (where the access road is). These small rocks represent the puppies of the adult wild dogs, and are regarded with particular affection by the custodians. Unfortunately they are very vulnerable to disturbance and there have been many instances where grief has been caused by the activities of earth-moving equipment. Some of the puppies can be seen at the back of Beaurepaires, and others around the base of Anzac Hill and by the road leading into Charles Creek community.

The puppies behind Beaurepaires.

The puppies at the base of Anzac Hill.

Billy Goat Hill and Anzac Hill, the two most prominent hills in the main town area, have been extensively used by Europeans but are also important sites. Many years ago, well before the era of consultation with Aboriginal people, water tanks were placed on both the hills. Recently, the government did approach the custodians, seeking their permission to remove the tanks, which were no longer used and were now seen as an eyesore. Permission was given. Predictably, the next step was an approach by the Town Council to enlarge the carpark on Anzac Hill, to include the area once covered by the tank. This was couched in terms of the safety of tourist buses and the like. How, in the long run, could the custodians refuse? You will note a large rock at the carpark entrance. This is a sacred rock, but since the carpark development the road shaves right past it. Approaches by companies wishing to build revolving restaurants on top of Billy Goat Hill have so far been resisted!

The Dreaming associations of Billy Goat Hill and Anzac Hill include two sisters as well as uninitiated boys, who travelled by on their way north to the Old Telegraph Station (OTS). These parties actually traversed great distances and engaged in a great deal of by-play, mainly of a flirtatious and humorous nature, although in the area of the OTS and certain other places their interaction became violent. If you look north from Anzac Hill, you will see a pair of hills which indicate the location of the

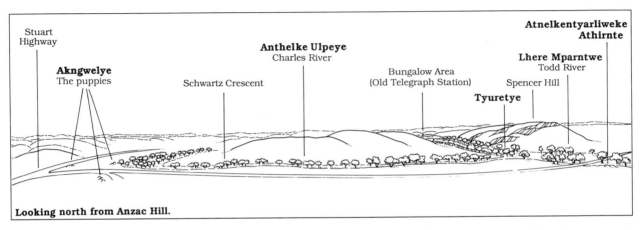

Stuart Highway

Akngwelye
The puppies

Anthelke Ulpeye
Charles River

Schwartz Crescent

Bungalow Area
(Old Telegraph Station)

Atnelkentyarliweke
Athirnte

Lhere Mparntwe
Todd River

Spencer Hill

Tyuretye

Looking north from Anzac Hill.

OTS. The area is rich in historical as well as mythological associations for Aboriginal people in Alice Springs. Most of the adult generation lived there for a time in the 1940's and 50's, when they were not permitted to enter the town area. Later the government decided to create the present historical reserve, and they shifted the Aboriginal people to another location much further away. Despite these circumstances, many people acquired particularly strong attachments to the OTS area, or 'The Bungalow' as it is known.

If you now trace the course of the Todd back towards town, you will see the point where it forms a junction with the smaller Charles River coming in from the west. This area is called **Tyuretye** (sometimes spelt Choritja) and is regarded as the real central point of Mparntwe. Not far from here is the Schwarz Crescent causeway, just south of which is the important rock in the river bed, **Atnelkentyarliweke Athirnte**, associated with the caterpillars. We will talk more about this in the next section.

ANNIE MEYER HILL

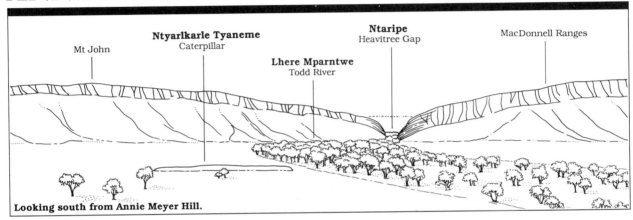

Mt John · Ntyarlkarle Tyaneme — Caterpillar · Lhere Mparntwe — Todd River · Ntaripe — Heavitree Gap · MacDonnell Ranges

Looking south from Annie Meyer Hill.

Climb the 'Sadadeen Walking Trail' within the Olive Pink Flora Reserve and go towards the south-western end of the hill, nearest the **Lhere Mparntwe** (Todd River). You will see an interpretive sign indicating the location of several Arrernte sites, some of which are also mentioned in this booklet. Find a spot which gives you a clear view of the valley between Annie Meyer Hill and the main MacDonnell Range due south (Mt John).

You will recall that after leaving their home at **Anthwerrke** (Emily Gap) the caterpillar beings swarmed over the country on this side of the Todd River. Emily Gap, the next break in the main range to the east of Heavitree Gap, and a vitally important site for the whole region, is just out of view from where you stand.

One of the first sites created by the Ntyarlke caterpillars in their travels was **Ntyarlkarle Tyaneme**. This is a small ridge running east-west parallel to the line of dark green roofs (the Desert Palms Motel) in the middle distance. Topographically and mythologically, the ridge is connected with a number of similar rises on the valley floor to the east, through the golf course area. The name of the site tells that the ridge was a point at which the caterpillars crossed the river.

The caterpillar at Barrett Drive.

You will notice a road at right angles to the ridge, passing between

15

it and the river. (This road, called Barrett Drive, forms a major T-junction below where you are standing.) When Barrett Drive was being planned the valley contained few of the new-look houses which stand there now. Only the Casino was there: it is the complex of triangular-roofed buildings visible beyond the Desert Palms.

In 1983 the government began to construct Barrett Drive in order to facilitate access to the Casino. They had a problem: Ntarlkarle Tyaneme, registered and protected under their own Aboriginal Sacred Sites Act, extended into the desired path of the road. Discussions ensued with the Aboriginal custodians. It appeared that the only way to avoid the site was by creating a deviation in the road, and the planners could not agree to that. There was a suggestion that the ground might be built up on either side of the ridge to make a hump, thus covering part of the site but not disturbing it. While far from reconciled to this idea, the custodians were considering it.

So far so good. At least the government was trying to find a solution. And they had promised to take no action until a resolution was reached.

Then at Christmas 1983 one of the custodians happened to walk out to the spot (vehicle access to the area had been restricted for some time because of the larger roadworks). He saw that the tail of the caterpillar was missing. The government, running out of patience, had sought to take advantage of the quiet holiday time and had ordered the dynamiting and bulldozing of the ridge. Barrett Drive has become known as Broken Promise Drive among the Arrernte people of Mparntwe, and the incident is one of the most bitterly felt of recent years. (Yet, apart from a few officials and workers immediately involved, the white community of Alice Springs hardly knows about it – and unfortunately this is indicative of a general lack of awareness about Aboriginal matters.)

Charges were laid under the Sacred Sites Act against the Minister for Lands and others responsible, but were later dropped when it was found that the Act was not binding on the Crown.

Other agreements were also made in the mid-1980's about development in this locality (the Mt John valley) which is now marketed as the prestige residential as well as tourist area of Alice Springs. The thrust to all of the negotiations from an Aboriginal point of view has been to try and stop or restrict development on the hills and rises. Their success can be judged from time to time by changes in the view from

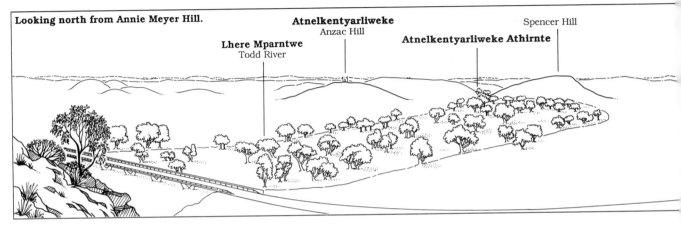

Looking north from Annie Meyer Hill.

Lhere Mparntwe
Todd River

Atnelkentyarliweke
Anzac Hill

Atnelkentyarliweke Athirnte

Spencer Hill

the spot at which you now stand.

If you now cross to the northern side of Annie Meyer Hill, you will have an excellent view of the remainder of Alice Springs' east side. Orientate yourself by reference to Anzac Hill, topped by its white R.S.L. memorial. In the Sadadeen Valley below you there are two major roads; Stott Terrace which extends from the bridge in a curve to the north, and Sadadeen Road which forms a T-junction with it and then heads eastward.

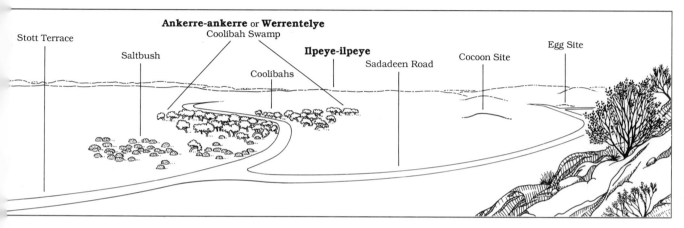

If you focus now on the area either side of the curve in Stott Terrace you will notice that there is an extensive stand of large trees. These are coolibah or box trees, and they are noticeably different from the river red gums growing in the Todd River bed. Old man saltbush is growing amongst them and the soil in the area is white with salt. It is characteristic of central Australia to find such swampy coolibah stands on the flood plains out from the banks of larger creeks.

At this swamp (**Ankerre Ankerre** or **Werrentelye**), a bout of dancing, ceremonies

19

Coolibah swamp.

of a public nature and other celebrations occurred in the Creative period, involving the local Yeperenye caterpillars and a group of their counterparts from **Urlatherrke**, Mt Zeil, a hundred kilometres away in the western MacDonnell Ranges.

The construction of Stott Terrace and of drains through the suburbs have of course completely altered the water flow patterns. There was consultation with custodians in the planning of this road. What happened though was that the necessity for a road through the swamp was presented to the custodians as a fait accompli — they could really only influence the exact alignment. They chose a route that involved cutting down the least number of trees.

20

One of the first places visited by the Mt Zeil 'mob' of caterpillars when they came to Alice Springs was a famous rock outcrop in the Todd River bed called **Atnelkentyarliweke Athirnte**. This rock represents the caterpillars who camped here overnight and ate Ayepe vine, their characteristic food. They also painted themselves and established the ceremonial law by which future people could ensure the continuance of the species.

The older Arrernte people of Alice Springs remember how, in the early days of the town, this rock was always kept covered by river sand so that it would not be seen by women and uninitiated men.

If you look for the Schwartz Crescent causeway which crosses the river in the far distance, the site is just this side of it, near the western bank. The rock is linked physically and mythologically with an outcrop on the bank nearby, and this in turn is linked with Anzac Hill, one of the names of which is also **Atnelkentyarliweke.**

Several years ago the site of one of Alice Springs' well-known white people's annual festivals, the Henley-on-Todd, was shifted downstream, closer to the causeway, because of Aboriginal concern about the exposure of the rock to large numbers of people. When the caterpillars moved on from this site, they visited a number of places in the Sadadeen Valley. One place is marked by an individual old tree at the base of Spencer Hill, the prominent hill in the middle of your view. Immediately to the north of the Ankerre Ankerre swamp there used to be a low sandy hill where they paused to rest as the sun rose, and were first seen by the local caterpillar mob. This hill has disappeared under a sporting club-house.

Cocoon site.

East of the swamp, between the water-slide and the big shed of the Y.M.C.A., is a small hill which is a caterpillar cocoon site, while the whitish gravel comprising the caterpillar egg site can be seen in the distance along Sadadeen Road.

Hills fringing Sadadeen Valley from the east to the north are all connected with the caterpillars, as is the hill on which you are standing. The valley was much used until a few decades ago for ceremonies, and for hunting and gathering of plant food. A soakage **Ilpeye Ilpeye** on the north-east edge of the valley was an important camping place, but has now been obliterated. A plaque on a lump of rock in a little suburban street called Nardoo Court records this fact.

Egg site.

The names of some of the more distant peaks that you see on the horizon, from both here and Anzac Hill, were recorded by Spencer and Gillen in their book. Many of these places are beyond the Mparntwe region and traditionally belonged to different descent groups. Few members of these groups are now alive, though because of inter-marriage, custodianship of the places has been maintained, in some cases by Mparntwe people. It is a remarkable fact that despite the enormous impact of the town, the people whose country was affected the most have survived. Not only have they survived but in many ways they are flourishing, as can be seen in their determination to protect their sites and also in the work undertaken in other spheres by their organisations around the town. We hope this booklet conveys a sense of what this courageous group faces in trying to defend itself against the continuing 'damaging of the dreaming land'. And we trust that the landscape springs to life a little more for the reader, as a result of the meanings and stories related here.

References:

Rowell, M. 1981, 'Sacred Sites Requiring Immediate Protection in the Alice Springs Area: A Preliminary Report on Consultations with Women Traditional Owners.' Unpublished report lodged with Aboriginal Sacred Sites Protection Authority.

Spencer, B. and Gillen, F.J. 1927, *The Arunta*, MacMillan and Company Limited, London.

Stevens, T. 1984, *Damaging Our Dreaming Land*, Yipirinya School Literacy Production Centre.